Growth Mindset Parenting
Inspiring Resiliency and Progress

Table of Contents

1. Introduction 1
2. Understanding a Growth Mindset: The Backbone of Resilience . . . 2
    2.1. An Overview of a Growth Mindset 2
    2.2. The Cornerstones of a Growth Mindset 3
    2.3. Encouraging a Growth Mindset: The Role of Praise 4
    2.4. The Fruit of a Growth Mindset: Resilience 4
    2.5. Fostering a Growth Mindset in Children: The Power of "Yet" . . 4
3. The Influence of Parents: Power-Shapers of a Child's Mindset 6
    3.1. The Power of Active Parenting 6
    3.2. Scaffolding the Growth Mindset 7
    3.3. Establishing a Safe Emotional Environment 7
    3.4. Inspiring Personal Development and Self-Efficacy 8
    3.5. The Impact of Parents' Mindset 8
4. Parental Strategies for Developing a Growth Mindset 10
    4.1. The Power of Affirmative Language 10
    4.2. Embracing Errors 11
    4.3. Nurturing Curiosity 11
    4.4. Setting the Right Expectations 11
    4.5. Encouraging Goal Setting 12
    4.6. Facilitating a Resourceful Environment 12
5. A Step-by-step Guide to Growth Mindset Conversation 14
    5.1. Identifying a Fixed Mindset 14
    5.2. Transitioning to a Growth Mindset 14
    5.3. Implementing a Growth Mindset 15
    5.4. Incorporating Growth Mindset Conversations into Everyday Life 16
6. The Role of Failure in Promoting Resilience: An Essential Lesson 18

- 6.1. Embracing the Notion of Failure … 18
- 6.2. Lessons From Notable Personalities … 18
- 6.3. Instilling the Growth Mindset … 19
- 6.4. Learning from Failures: Putting Theory into Practice … 19
- 6.5. Nurturing Emotional Resilience … 20
- 6.6. The Power of Parental Role Modeling … 20
- 7. Nurturing Natural Curiosity: The Essential Ingredient for Progress … 22
  - 7.1. The Vital Role of Curiosity … 22
  - 7.2. Understanding the Underpinnings of Curiosity … 22
  - 7.3. Breathing Life into Curiosity … 23
  - 7.4. Curiosity and the Growth Mindset … 23
  - 7.5. Guiding but not Governing … 24
  - 7.6. The Endless Cycle of Questions … 24
  - 7.7. Curiosity is the Start; Persistence is the Key … 24
- 8. Embracing Challenges: Placing Effort above Talent … 26
  - 8.1. Developing a Growth Mindset: Understanding its Core … 26
  - 8.2. The Art of Praising: Encourage Effort Over Ability … 26
  - 8.3. Transform Errors into Teachable Moments … 27
  - 8.4. Design Challenges that Foster Growth … 27
  - 8.5. Creating a Growth-Inspired Household … 28
  - 8.6. In Conclusion … 28
- 9. Cultivating a Love for Learning: Key to Enduring Progress … 30
  - 9.1. Why a Love for Learning Matters … 30
  - 9.2. Incorporating a Growth Mindset: The Foundation of a Love for Learning … 31
  - 9.3. Fostering a Growth Mindset at Home: Practical Strategies … 31
  - 9.4. Cultivating Curiosity: A Precursor to a Love for Learning … 32
- 10. Practical Growth Mindset Activities for Home and School … 34
  - 10.1. Making Growth Mindset Tangible at Home … 34

    10.2. Activities that Foster Growth Mindset in Schools 34
    10.3. The Power of Constructive Feedback 35
    10.4. Mindfulness and Growth Mindset. 35
    10.5. Applying Growth Mindset in Real Life 36
    10.6. Challenge and the Growth Mindset. 36
11. Strengthening the Parent-Child Bond: The Emotional Aspects
of Growth Mindset. 37
    11.1. The Emotional Landscape of Children 37
    11.2. Building Emotional Intelligence. 38
    11.3. Empathy: A Powerful Tool. 38
    11.4. Facilitating Healthy Emotional Expression 39
    11.5. Reflection and Emotional Growth. 40

Chapter 1. Introduction

Ready to embark on an empowering journey that scaffolds your child's hidden potentials? Our Special Report on 'Growth Mindset Parenting: Inspiring Resiliency and Progress' offers invaluable insights and practical strategies to mold a resilient, adaptive, and progress-friendly mindset in your children. This captivating guide, filled with research-backed parenting practices, nuanced understanding of child psychology, and real-life applications, promises to revolutionize your parenting techniques and nurture true resilience in your child. Don't miss the opportunity to unlock a future of boundless possibilities for your child. Order this eye-opening Special Report now and let vibrant growth take root in your family!

Chapter 2. Understanding a Growth Mindset: The Backbone of Resilience

The journey to cultivating a growth mindset begins with understanding the very essence of what it means to possess this invaluable perspective. A growth mindset is the belief that one's abilities, intelligence, and talents can be improved over time through dedication, effort, and challenges. This fundamental perception contrasts with a static mindset, or the belief that these attributes are inherent and unalterable.

Adopting a growth mindset doesn't necessarily mean insisting that anyone could become anything they want with enough dedication and hard work. Instead, it's about opening oneself up to constant learning and believing in the potential to develop and refine one's abilities. An individual with a growth mindset acknowledges that personal development isn't solely contingent upon natural inclination or inherent talent but rather on continued learning, resilience, and dedication.

2.1. An Overview of a Growth Mindset

Dr. Carol Dweck, a renowned psychologist and researcher at Stanford University, introduced the groundbreaking concepts of "fixed mindset" and "growth mindset." According to Dr. Dweck's research, those with a fixed mindset believe their intelligence and abilities are fixed traits that can't be changed. Consequently, these individuals often avoid challenges, give up easily when met with obstacles, and view effort as futile or even threatening. In sharp contrast, individuals with a growth mindset relish in challenges, persist in the face of setbacks, see effort as a path to mastery, and learn from criticism.

It's crucial to note that the human brain is innately capable of learning and adapting, indicating that a shift from a fixed mindset to a growth mindset is entirely possible. Neuroplasticity, the brain's inherent ability to change and adapt as a result of experience, paves the way to cultivating a growth mindset. Thus, anyone, regardless of age, can shift their outlook from seeing intelligence as a fixed entity to understanding it as a malleable attribute that can develop over time.

2.2. The Cornerstones of a Growth Mindset

A growth mindset is constructed on several fundamental beliefs and attitudes that shape how one interprets failure, criticism, effort, and success.

1. **Embracing Challenges**: People with a growth mindset see challenges as opportunities for self-improvement rather than threats to their self-worth.
2. **Resilience in the Face of Setbacks**: Mistakes, failures, and obstacles are perceived not as defining characteristics but as steppingstones for improvement and growth.
3. **The Importance of Effort**: Effort is viewed as a necessary attribute for success rather than a last resort reserved for tasks that lie beyond one's capabilities.
4. **The Power of Feedback and Criticism**: Constructive feedback and criticism are embraced as valuable tools for personal growth.
5. **The Joy of Success in Others**: Rather than feeling threatened by the success of peers and colleagues, those with a growth mindset find it inspiring and informative.

2.3. Encouraging a Growth Mindset: The Role of Praise

Praise plays a profound role in shaping a child's mindset. Traditional methods of praise often focus on a child's innate abilities, such as being smart or talented. While this may boost their self-esteem momentarily, it inadvertently encourages a fixed mindset. Evidence suggests that praising efforts, strategies, and perseverance fosters a growth mindset, emphasizing the role of hard work and ongoing learning in achieving success.

2.4. The Fruit of a Growth Mindset: Resilience

Resilience, or the capacity to bounce back from adversity, failure, or even trauma, is deeply intertwined with a growth mindset. Resilience isn't about avoiding difficulty, but rather learning to cope with it, bounce back quickly, and come out stronger on the other side. A child equipped with a growth mindset sees failure as a mere temporary setback on their path to progress, and thus, they persist, learn, and adapt, nurturing their innate resiliency.

2.5. Fostering a Growth Mindset in Children: The Power of "Yet"

Dr. Dweck proposes a powerful tool in guiding children towards a growth mindset: the power of "yet." When children say they can't do something, adding the word "yet" at the end switches the narrative from one of defeat to one of potential. This simple linguistic shift can have profound implications, helping children realize that their abilities aren't fixed and can improve over time with consistent effort and patience.

In conclusion, understanding a growth mindset is the first, pivotal step towards cultivating resilience and fostering a love for learning, both in ourselves and our children. By recognizing potential as variable and building upon failure rather than fearing it, we can embolden our children to strive persistently, embrace challenges assertively, and grow exponentially, reaping the lifelong benefits of a growth mindset. The road ahead is a promising one, full of opportunities to learn, persist, and thrive.

Chapter 3. The Influence of Parents: Power-Shapers of a Child's Mindset

Parents exert a tremendous influence on their children's mindset from early childhood through adolescence and beyond. Even before they can speak, children pick up on their parents' attitudes and behaviors, creating a strong foundation for their own views on the world.

3.1. The Power of Active Parenting

Active parenting is when parents consciously cultivate a particular mindset or set of skills in their children rather than simply reacting to problematic behaviors. By being proactive, parents can help their children form a positive self-image, encouraging them to be resilient and to believe in their ability to grow and learn from challenges.

The way parents talk to their children plays a crucial role in instilling a growth mindset. For example, praising effort rather than innate talent emphasizes the importance of working hard and trying new strategies, fostering a growth mindset. On the other hand, labeling a child as "smart" or "gifted" may inadvertently create the idea that intelligence is a fixed trait, leading to a static mindset.

Parents can also encourage a growth mindset by being a role model. Demonstrating a passion for learning, embracing challenges, persevering in the face of setbacks, and viewing effort as a path to mastery can all help instill these growth-oriented values in a child.

3.2. Scaffolding the Growth Mindset

Scaffolding refers to the support that parents provide to help their children reach a higher level of understanding or skill. This could be in the form of emotional support, such as encouraging words, or practical assistance, like helping a child solve a difficult puzzle.

The concept of scaffolding is particularly relevant for developing a growth mindset. Parents can provide scaffolding in the form of strategies for overcoming challenges, helping children see mistakes as learning opportunities rather than signs of failure.

This could involve breaking down a complex task into manageable parts, modeling how to solve problems, or providing feedback that focuses on the process rather than the outcome. By doing so, parents can help their children move from a fixed to a growth mindset, enhancing their ability to overcome challenges and persist in the face of obstacles.

3.3. Establishing a Safe Emotional Environment

Parents can also influence their child's mindset by creating a safe emotional environment. Children are more likely to develop a growth mindset in an environment that allows them to express their emotions, grants them the freedom to make mistakes, and provides encouragement and constructive feedback.

To foster such an environment, parents can work on developing their own emotional intelligence, allowing them to understand and respond to their children's emotional needs effectively. They can also focus on providing unconditional love, support, and positive reinforcement regardless of their child's achievements or failures.

3.4. Inspiring Personal Development and Self-Efficacy

Another way parents can encourage a growth mindset is by fostering their child's personal development and self-efficacy. Building self-efficacy refers to helping children believe in their abilities to complete tasks and achieve goals.

Parents can promote self-efficacy by setting achievable goals and helping their children devise plans to accomplish them. Moreover, allowing children to make decisions and take responsibility for their actions can also boost their confidence and independence.

Ultimately, inspiring personal development helps children realize that their abilities and intelligence can grow with effort and time.

3.5. The Impact of Parents' Mindset

Finally, parents should be aware of how their own mindset can affect their children's perception and approach towards life. Parents with a fixed mindset might unknowingly impose their beliefs onto their children, leading them to adopt a similar attitude towards their abilities and potential.

In contrast, parents who embrace a growth mindset can pass on the same values to their children, fostering resilience, adaptability, and a love for learning. This influence extends far beyond academic performance; it enriches children's interpersonal relationships, their ability to cope with stress, and their overall mental well-being.

In closing, parents wield significant power in shaping their children's mindset. By adopting conscious parenting strategies and cultivating a growth mindset, parents can empower their children to reach their potential, deal resiliently with life's challenges, and establish a lifelong love for learning - equipping them with the mindset to chart an inspiring course in life. The journey might be filled with ebbs and flows, but it promises a rewarding destination.

Chapter 4. Parental Strategies for Developing a Growth Mindset

Do your children see challenges as threats or opportunities? The lens through which they view these situations profoundly impacts their resilience and adaptability, shaping their futures. The first step is to understand the underlying fabric of a 'growth mindset,' which embraces the belief that skills and intelligence can be developed progressively. This philosophy hinges on the power of 'yet,' turning 'I can't do it' into 'I can't do it yet.' Here's how you can foster this mindset in your child.

4.1. The Power of Affirmative Language

Words have the power to shape realities. The language you use can either foster a fixed or growth mindset in your child. So, it's imperative to mind your language, using affirmative words that strengthen your child's self-efficacy, positively impacting their attitude towards learning and challenges.

Avoid tag lines such as 'genius,' 'brilliant,' or 'incredibly smart,' which reinforce a fixed mindset. Instead, encourage effort, strategy, and persistence. Awarding hard work, concentration, perseverance, and creativity fosters a growth mindset.

Remember, problem-solving requires a blend of effort, strategy, and resilience. So, instead of saying, "You're a genius," use phrases that anticipate progress such as, "I liked how you persisted on that task," or, "That's a clever strategy you applied there."

4.2. Embracing Errors

Many consider mistakes and failures as the end of the road. But a change in perspective can redefine these errors as stepping stones to success, reinforcing a growth mindset. Christian Dweck, a renowned psychologist, said, "Mistakes are our friends. They help us grow".

Not only can you promote this perspective, but you can also demonstrate it through your own actions. When you make a mistake, openly acknowledge it, analyze its root cause, and discuss how to rectify it in the future.

When your child stumbles, resist the urge to swoop in and fix their problems. Instead, guide them towards a solution. This strategy fosters resilience, making them more adaptive and open to learning.

4.3. Nurturing Curiosity

Curiosity is at the root of a growth mindset, harboring an innate desire to learn and grow. Encourage your child's curiosity by asking thought-provoking questions and valuing their queries. This practice helps them develop critical thinking skills and a love for learning.

A supportive environment that values curiosity acts as fertile ground for a growth mindset. It can be as simple as asking, "What is your strategy?" or, "What can we learn from this?" to scaffold their learning ability.

4.4. Setting the Right Expectations

It's essential to establish that perseverance and effort are as significant as the final result. Reward the process, emphasize learning from mistakes, and ensure that they are comfortable with the idea of growth from failure. This strategy promotes an orientation towards growth and increases their willingness to step outside their comfort zone, paving the way for progress and development.

Shifting from a performance-driven to a growth-oriented approach also nurtures perseverance in your child. Instead of focusing only on outcomes, assigning tasks that require patience and resilience can reinforce their growth mindset.

4.5. Encouraging Goal Setting

Help your kids set achievable short-term and long-term goals to foster a sense of purpose, thus fueling their growth mindset. This practice not only enhances their motivation but also develops their planning and problem-solving skills.

Try guiding your child to break their goals down into manageable tasks that they can accomplish step-by-step. Celebrate as each step is completed. This method makes the objective seem more attainable, reducing fear of failure and building self-confidence.

4.6. Facilitating a Resourceful Environment

Finally, a conducive learning environment - rich with resources - acts as a catalyst in developing a growth mindset. Create spaces conducive to conversation, creativity, and curiosity at home. Surround your child with books, educational games, and puzzles to stimulate innovative thinking and foster intrinsic motivation to learn.

By implementing these strategies, you are doing more than encouraging good habits. You are building a framework that inspires a resilient, loving, and progress-friendly mindset, vital for your child's success. The framework ensures that every stumbling block becomes a stepping stone and every challenge becomes an opportunity - thus unlocking a future filled with opportunities for your children.

Chapter 5. A Step-by-step Guide to Growth Mindset Conversation

Understanding a child's mindset and encouraging a growth approach toward learning can be a transformative experience for both the parent and the child. Incorporating this approach into our daily conversations is a crucial part of helping our children realize their true potential. This comprehensive guide aims to equip parents with the knowledge and techniques necessary to encourage a growth mindset in their children, fostering resilience and progress through daily conversation.

5.1. Identifying a Fixed Mindset

Before you can change a child's mindset from fixed to growth, it's essential to recognize the characteristics of a fixed mindset. Children with a fixed mindset believe their basic abilities like intelligence and talent are static, leading them to avoid challenges, give up easily, and view effort as fruitless or worse. Success may be seen as a confirmation of inherent intelligence, and failure may become a fear that inhibits growth and learning. In your conversations, listen for these signs and prepare to gently guide the child towards a growth mindset.

5.2. Transitioning to a Growth Mindset

The next step is to start using certain techniques for instilling a growth mindset. Use growth mindset language, praise effort instead of intelligence, talk about the brain as a muscle that can get stronger with use, and discuss examples of people who succeeded through hard work and resilience.

- Growth Mindset Language: Incorporate phrases such as "You don't know this...yet" or "You're learning from your mistakes." This language encourages children to see their abilities as things that can be developed over time.
- Praising Effort: Use praise that commends effort, strategy, and improvement. Avoid linking success directly to qualities such as intelligence or talent. For example, instead of saying "You're so smart," you might say, "I can see how much effort you put into solving this problem."
- Brain as a Muscle: Discuss how the brain is like a muscle, growing and developing with use. Encourage your child to exercise their brain by embracing challenges.
- Discussing Examples: Talk about real-life examples of individuals who achieved great things through effort and perseverance. Using biographies can vividly illustrate these lessons.

Critical to this transition is the understanding that mistakes and challenges are not only inevitable but also beneficial. Encourage your children to view these as opportunities for growth, reinforcing on this concept through your conversations.

5.3. Implementing a Growth Mindset

With the foundations of a growth mindset in place, the next step involves incorporating this mindset into everyday life. Here, it's crucial to provide a supportive environment that encourages risk-taking and doesn't punish failure.

- Encourage Risk-Taking: Make a safe environment for your children to take risks. This can be as simple as trying a new food, learning a new sport, or attempting a challenging puzzle. Highlight the process, the risks involved, and the potential learnings, not the outcome.

- Embrace Failure: Teach children to view failure as part of the learning process rather than as a critique of their intelligence or talent. If they know it's okay to fail, they'll be more willing to take on challenges and grow.

- Model a Growth Mindset: Your own behavior is a powerful teaching tool. Model a growth mindset by talking about your own struggles and how you've learned and grown from them.

5.4. Incorporating Growth Mindset Conversations into Everyday Life

Finally, it's crucial to infuse everyday conversations with a growth mindset. This doesn't mean redefining your children's entire vocabulary. Instead, it involves asking open-ended questions to encourage learning and showing empathy when they struggle.

- Open-Ended Questions: These types of questions promote deep thinking and often lead to further investigation. For instance, questions like "How would you solve this problem differently next time?" or "What did you learn from this experience?"

- Empathy: Recognize and validate your child's feelings when they make mistakes or face challenges. Show that you understand their frustration and encourage them to persevere by gently guiding them to recognize the potential learning opportunities present.

Incorporating a growth mindset into your conversations is less about changing what you say and more about changing how you say it. Offering encouragement, discussing efforts and strategies, and praising progress over perfection are key. As time goes on, these growth mindset conversations can establish a lifetime's worth of resilience and progress.

Chapter 6. The Role of Failure in Promoting Resilience: An Essential Lesson

In our journey as parents, understanding the concept of failure and its symbiotic relationship with success plays a pivotal role in shaping a resilient mindset in our children. Contrary to popular belief, failure isn't the massive roadblock we often perceive it to be. It's a stepping stone in the learning process, an invaluable life lesson, and a catalyst for resilience, growth, and ultimately, success.

6.1. Embracing the Notion of Failure

In order to leverage failure as a tool for promoting resilience, we must first embrace it. The perspective that we carry about failure profoundly influences the way we relay its concept to our children. Teaching children to recognize failure as an essential cog in the wheel of learning enables them to mentally shift from a debilitating fear of failure to viewing it as a crucial part of progress.

Often, we attempt to shield our children from failure, perceiving it as inherently bad or damaging. However, it isn't the failure itself that can harm but how one reacts and learns from it that determines whether the experience becomes a stumbling block or a stepping stone. Resilient individuals see failure as an opportunity for growth, learning, and improvement.

6.2. Lessons From Notable Personalities

History and present times brim with stories of luminaries who have failed before they found success. Be it Abraham Lincoln's repeated failures before he became a prominent leader or Thomas Edison's string of unsuccessful experiments before inventing the light bulb; their narratives underscore the importance of resilience and underscore that persistence, despite perceived failures, is an undeniable route to success.

These inspirational stories can be an effective tool in teaching children about the value of failure, providing tangible evidence that failures are not only common but also a critical aspect of everyone's success journey.

6.3. Instilling the Growth Mindset

Stanford psychologist Carol Dweck's work on "growth mindset" is monumental in understanding how perceptions of failure can influence resilience. Dweck posits that individuals with a "fixed mindset" believe their abilities are stable and unchangeable - leading them to view failure as a reflection of their inability.

On the contrary, individuals with a "growth mindset" understand that abilities and intelligence can be honed and improved. Failures aren't seen as a testament to their limitations but as opportunities to grow and learn. As parents, cultivating a growth mindset in our children involves praising effort, improvement, perseverance, and strategies they used rather than focusing solely on accomplishments.

6.4. Learning from Failures: Putting Theory into Practice

Practical ways to imbibe this can range from encouraging your children to acknowledge their mistakes, to helping them understand what they could do differently next time. Rather than dwelling on what went wrong, spend time reflecting on the lessons learned.

Engage in dialogue centering around questions like, "What strategies seemed to work well, and which ones less so?" "What did you learn from this that you can apply in the future?"

The very act of actively learning from failures can enhance problem-solving skills, decision-making, promote a healthier approach to risk-taking, and boost self-confidence in the face of adversity - all key components in fostering resilience.

6.5. Nurturing Emotional Resilience

Another crucial aspect is teaching children to manage the emotions that surface from the experience of failure. Rather than suppress feelings of disappointment, frustration, or sadness, encourage them to acknowledge these emotions. This process invites open conversations about feelings and endorses a healthy expressivity that is vital to emotional resilience.

6.6. The Power of Parental Role Modeling

Remember, children look to their parents as role models. Therefore, being open about your own failures, emotional reactions, and the lessons learned, can serve as a powerful way to encourage your children towards a healthier approach to failure. When your child sees you bounce back from defeat, it reinforces their belief that they can overcome the challenges they face.

In conclusion, failure isn't something that eradicates potential; rather, it uncovers it. When embraced with a balanced understanding and perspective, it becomes more than just a negative outcome; it transforms into a powerful tool for resilience. This, bridled with a strong parental model that endorses a healthy attitude towards failure, can result in an empowered, resilient child ready to take on the world's challenges, learn, adapt and grow, regardless of the obstacles they encounter. Ultimately, it paves the way for a future infused with boundless possibilities where vibrant growth can indeed take root in your family.

Chapter 7. Nurturing Natural Curiosity: The Essential Ingredient for Progress

Curiosity is more than an innate trait; It's a spark that ignites our desire to learn, grow, and explore. As parents, one of the most valuable gifts we can give to our children is to nurture and nourish this sense of inquisitiveness. Together, let's discover how to do just that.

7.1. The Vital Role of Curiosity

Curiosity is the thirst for knowledge and understanding, a deep-seated desire to explore the world's mysteries. Children, endowed with an inherent sense of curiosity, often exhibit this trait by asking endless questions. From science to sports, no topic is off-limits to a curious child, and each question leads to another in a never-ending cycle of exploration

Scientifically, curiosity fires up the brain, stimulating growth and forging connections. Psychologically, it fosters a love for learning, driving children into a cycle of exploration, discovery, and delight. Emotionally, it develops resilience, teaching them to accept setbacks as stepping-stones to greater understanding.

7.2. Understanding the Underpinnings of Curiosity

While curiosity is inherent, its true power comes from sustained nurturing. Every 'why', 'how', or 'what' from a child is a golden opportunity. So how can we recognize and cultivate these moments?

The first step lies in understanding the underpinnings of curiosity.

In 1974, psychologist Daniel Berlyne proposed that curiosity could be divided into two types: perceptual and epistemic. Perceptual curiosity is sparked by novel, complex, and uncertain elements in our environment, while epistemic curiosity stems from a deep desire to learn and understand. By fostering both types, we can cultivate an environment conducive to curiosity.

7.3. Breathing Life into Curiosity

An environment fostering curiosity is one that is safe, stimulating, supportive, and open to asking and exploring the hundreds of questions that flood a child's mind. This environment can be achieved both physically, in terms of an interesting and playful environment, and psychologically, through open discussion and encouragement of fresh perspectives.

Hands-on activities, open-ended toys, books that challenge their understanding, outdoors exploration - all contribute to creating a stimulating environment. Similarly, answering with patience, encouraging debate, dealing with confusion constructively, and treating every question as valid lays down a fertile ground for questioning minds.

7.4. Curiosity and the Growth Mindset

Nurturing curiosity is seamlessly connected to fostering a growth mindset. Curiosity promotes learning, exploration, and discovery, all hallmarks of a growth mindset. It also equips children to manage failure and persist despite setbacks.

In essence, a curious child is one who views setbacks not as failures but as opportunities to learn more. This visionary perspective is quintessentially that of a growth mindset, aligning curiosity with resilience, adaptability, and progress.

7.5. Guiding but not Governing

While nurturing curiosity, a common pitfall can be excessive interference. While guiding and supporting can be beneficial, taking control over every exploration can dampen their enthusiasm to discover and learn. It's crucial to allow your child the freedom to stumble, question, and understand at their own pace.

7.6. The Endless Cycle of Questions

Children's questions can sometimes be relentless, exhausting and, frankly, annoying. But these questions show a keen desire to learn. Every question is a sign of their growing brains wanting to make sense of the world around them. In fact, viewing these questions from a different lens not merely as queries but opportunities to nourish and bolster their growing understanding – it can transform your perspective and strengthen your patience and commitment as a parent.

7.7. Curiosity is the Start; Persistence is the Key

Nurturing curiosity might be the first step, but teaching persistence or 'grit' is equally crucial. To maximize the benefits of curiosity, children need to persist in their explorations. This persistence, often referred to as 'grit', ensures that curiosity doesn't wane but persists, contributing to lifelong learning.

In summary, nurturing curiosity is an essential ingredient for a growth mindset. It's a long and rewarding journey, guiding and growing along with your child. While no single strategy is the 'perfect' one, a blend of encouragement, patience, understanding, and fostering a safe and stimulating environment will carve a unique parental path for you. Embrace this journey, and your child will embrace a better understanding of the world - a future full of boundless curiosity and unlimited possibilities.

Chapter 8. Embracing Challenges: Placing Effort above Talent

Parents have always emphasized the importance of talent, often putting it above all else. However, this conventional wisdom may not be as helpful as it seems. Research has shown that placing value on effort, rather than inherent talent, can lead to greater resilience in the face of challenges. Adopting an approach that underscores effort rather than talent facilitates a 'Growth Mindset', a term coined by psychologist Carol Dweck.

8.1. Developing a Growth Mindset: Understanding its Core

The growth mindset, as opposed to a fixed mindset, fosters the belief that abilities can be nurtured and developed through dedication and hard work. In contrast, a fixed mindset harbors the belief that abilities and intelligence are fixed traits, unable to be changed or improved.

By promoting a growth mindset, parents can encourage children to view mistakes and challenges as opportunities for growth, rather than insurmountable roadblocks. It emphasizes the importance of effort, teaching children that perseverance in the face of adversity is a strength, not a weakness.

8.2. The Art of Praising: Encourage Effort Over Ability

Praise can be a powerful motivator for children, but it's important to be mindful about the type of praise we give. Instead of praising children for their innate abilities (e.g., "Wow, you're so smart!"), parents should strive to recognize and celebrate their effort, strategies, and progress.

Research conducted by Dweck and her colleagues found that children who were praised for their effort ("I can see you worked really hard on this") were more likely to develop a growth mindset. These children understood that their effort led to success, and they tended to value learning and improvement over getting the right answer on the first try.

8.3. Transform Errors into Teachable Moments

Mistakes, failure, and hardship - while inherently challenging and often disappointing - are vital in the process of learning and growth. They are not experiences to be punished but should instead be exploited as teachable moments.

Parents who facilitate a growth mindset in their children present failures as opportunities to learn. Instead of focusing on the negative aspects of a failed attempt, they help their child identify what was learned and how they can improve in the future. This approach redirects the child's focus from the stigma of failure to the potential it holds for learning and progress.

8.4. Design Challenges that Foster Growth

To cultivate a growth mindset, it's critical to provide children with challenges that stretch their abilities, nudging them out of their comfort zones. These challenges can fuel ambition, promote problem-solving skills, and motivate children to strive for progress rather than perfection.

By designing these kinds of challenges, parents can offer children a safe space to fail, learn, and improve. For example, if your child has a knack for maths but struggles with narrative writing, encourage them to write a short story or a diary entry. This task, while difficult, will stimulate growth and underscore the importance of effort-driven improvement.

8.5. Creating a Growth-Inspired Household

A shift towards a growth mindset can - and should - permeate beyond individual attitudes to encompass the overall household environment. Display symbols of effort, growth, and progress throughout the home. Celebrate effort, hard work, and perseverance instead of innate talent or success.

Moreover, use inspirational stories – historical figures, family anecdotes, or well-known icons – who overcame failure, worked hard, and achieved success. These tales can be critical touchstones, illustrating the power of resilience and effort.

8.6. In Conclusion

Embracing challenges and placing effort above talent is a robust strategy for nurturing resilience and progress in children. By implementing these strategies, parents can help their children learn that intelligence and abilities are not fixed traits, but qualities that can grow and improve with effort, resilience, and determination. Remember, developing a growth mindset is a lifelong journey, and every step in the right direction fosters invaluable growth and resilience for the future.

With patience, understanding, and dedication, this journey can pave the way for children to experience a future filled with unlimited possibilities. Developing a child's growth mindset empowers them to embrace challenges head-on and encourages a lifelong passion for learning and growth. With every challenge they meet, they will be not only learning a new skill or gaining knowledge but also building the resilience they need for future challenges in life.

Chapter 9. Cultivating a Love for Learning: Key to Enduring Progress

Every parent yearns to see their child continuously flourish, both acadically and personally. One crucial aspect of this lifelong development is nurturing a love for learning, a factor that plays an integral role in bolstering enduring progress throughout life. This chapter will delve into the importance of inculcating this passion and provide practical strategies to foster it in your young ones.

9.1. Why a Love for Learning Matters

Enthusiasm for acquiring knowledge is more than just an admirable trait — it's the cornerstone of lifelong success. Embracing learning helps students approach their school years with a positive perspective, ready to absorb new concepts. More importantly, it extends beyond the classroom, shaping their self-improvement journey well into adulthood.

Research has consistently demonstrated the impressive effects of possessing an authentic love for learning. Learners with this attribute often showcase a higher level of engagement in their studies, leading to improved academic performance. Additionally, they tend to develop advanced problem-solving skills, demonstrating exceptional critical thinking abilities in varying situations.

Fostering a love for learning in a child not only expands their intellectual horizons but also strengthens their resolve in challenging situations. When children are imbued with this love, they more readily persist through difficulties, displaying resilience that helps them learn from setbacks rather than being disheartened by them.

9.2. Incorporating a Growth Mindset: The Foundation of a Love for Learning

At the heart of cultivating this love for learning is the pivotal concept of a growth mindset. Embodied by the belief that abilities and skills can be developed through dedication and hard work, a growth mindset contrasts sharply with a fixed mindset — the notion that our intelligence and talents are innate and unchangeable.

Carol Dweck, a prominent psychologist at Stanford University, has conducted extensive on the transformative impact of adopting a growth mindset. According to her research, individuals with a growth mindset often exhibit a love for learning and resilience that is crucial for lifetime achievement.

For children, adopting a growth mindset stimulates a sense of curiosity and a desire to understand the world around them. This mindset encourages the belief that with dedicated effort, they can continuously learn and progress. It transforms challenges into opportunities for learning and growth, helping children view mistakes not as failures, but as stepping stones to improvement.

9.3. Fostering a Growth Mindset at Home: Practical Strategies

There are numerous strategies that parents can employ to nurture a growth mindset in their children, thereby instigating a passion for learning.

1. **Praise Effort Over Outcome**: Believe in praising the process

rather than the result. Complimenting your child's efforts rather than merely their achievements helps establish that persistence and hard work are just as valuable as the end result.

2. **Model a Growth Mindset**: Children often learn by observing their role models — their parents. Showcase growth mindset behaviors in your own life. Show them your own learning process, your mistakes, and how you learn from them, fostering a positive attitude towards learning and growth.

3. **Encourage Curiosity**: Welcome questions and engage in exploratory discussions, providing space for your child to express their thoughts. This will promote a sense of wonderment, stimulating their desire to learn more about the world around them.

4. **Promote Goal Setting**: Encourage your child to set academic and personal goals. Teach them that goals are markers of progress, not measures of success or failure. Goals will motivate them to continuously learn and grow, leading them towards their desired achievements.

5. **Reframe Challenges as Opportunities**: Teach your children to view difficulties as opportunities to learn, thus enabling them to embrace challenging tasks rather than shy away from them.

9.4. Cultivating Curiosity: A Precursor to a Love for Learning

Curiosity, an integral part of a love for learning, is the inner spark that drives the quest for knowledge and understanding. It is the profound desire to know, to explore, to understand, that fuels constant learning. Inquisitive by nature, children are innate explorers. Encouraging inquisitiveness and curiosity will instigate a constant quest for knowledge, thereby reinforcing a love for learning.

You can foster curiosity in children by promoting exploration and discovery. Allow your children to delve into their interests and passions, providing them with the resources to explore their curiosity. Encourage questions, embrace their wonderment, and be open to learning together.

Furthermore, introducing children to diverse topics, ideas, and cultures can stimulate their intellectual curiosity. This exposure can expand their horizons, spur new interests, and thus, kindle a passion for learning.

By effectively incorporating these strategies and fostering a cherishing curiosity in your child, you set them on a path towards an enduring love for learning. This love will not only guide them in their academic pursuits but also facilitate their personal growth throughout life. It's about enabling young minds to realize their potential and creating lifelong learners ready to face the future with confidence and resilience.

Remember, the journey of learning forever continues. As a parent, you have the unique opportunity to nurture this zeal for learning in your child — a gift that will continue to bear fruit throughout their life. By equipping your child with a love for learning, you are shaping them into adaptable, proactive individuals, ready to thrive in a ceaselessly evolving world.

Chapter 10. Practical Growth Mindset Activities for Home and School

10.1. Making Growth Mindset Tangible at Home

Home is where your child's learning begins, and it's an optimal space to plant seeds of a growth mindset. Several activities can reinforce resilience and progress.

A highly beneficial and fun-filled activity is the 'Effort Jar.' You could use a simple glass jar with a lid and within this jar, acknowledge your child's efforts rather than their outcomes. Every time your child tries something new or pushes themselves out of their comfort zone, write this event on a piece of paper and place it in the jar. Over time, this jar will fill up and become a physical evidence of your child's relentless efforts and resilience.

Additionally, you can establish a 'Growth Mindset Wall.' On a blank wall or bulletin board, you can stick pictures, quotes, or stories that inspire a growth mindset, or display drawings your child has made to depict their understanding of the idea. The visual reminder can keep the growth mindset principles alive and integrate them organically into your child's daily life.

10.2. Activities that Foster Growth Mindset in Schools

School plays a crucial role in your child's development, and incorporating specific activities can encourage a growth mindset in this setting. One of the practices is 'Two Stars and a Wish.' After your child completes a school project, point out two things they did well (stars) and one area where they can improve (wish). This approach not only builds their resilience but also motivates them to strive for better outcomes.

The 'Growth Vs. Fixed Mindset Role Plays' can provide a dynamic method for students to understand these concepts. Children can act out scenarios associated with growth and fixed mindsets, thus helping them identify the difference between the two and realize the importance of a growth mindset.

10.3. The Power of Constructive Feedback

Both at home and school, a well-structured feedback plays a key part in developing a growth mindset. It's essential to focus on the process rather than the end result. For instance, instead of saying, "You are so smart," try "I'm proud of how hard you worked on this task." This subtle shift emphasizes effort, strategizing and persistence, underscoring that intellect and ability can be developed.

10.4. Mindfulness and Growth Mindset

Mindfulness activities help build an awareness of the here and now, centering children's attention on their current feelings, thoughts, and actions. This focus on the present moment complements the growth mindset by making children more conscious of their learning processes and effective strategies.

Mindfulness activities may include child-friendly meditation, yoga or simple breathing exercises. Practiced routinely, these tools can help children better manage stress, enhance their concentration, and foster a growth mindset by becoming more aware of their mental processes.

10.5. Applying Growth Mindset in Real Life

Regular reflecting on real-life situations can be an excellent exercise in developing a growth mindset. Whether it's dissecting the success of a favorite sportsperson or understanding failures of famous inventors, discussing how they've used a growth mindset can illuminate the power of resilience and progress. This can ignite inspiration and provide your child with relatable examples.

10.6. Challenge and the Growth Mindset

Learning to respond positively to challenges is a central aspect of the growth mindset. At home and school, children can be given controlled, achievable challenges that encourage them to step out of comfort zones. Such experiences can help teach valuable lessons about patience, perseverance, staying motivated, and embracing the learning process.

A growth mindset isn't an overnight transformation; it's a journey filled with small, consistent, and intentional actions. As parents and educators, you have the chance to mold this journey and equip your child with the tools they need to navigate the world with a resilient and progress-oriented mindset. Through these interactive activities and a rooted understanding of growth mindset principles, you can create an encouraging, dynamic environment that promotes your child's inherent potential.

Chapter 11. Strengthening the Parent-Child Bond: The Emotional Aspects of Growth Mindset

Forging a positive relationship with your child plays a paramount role in facilitating growth mindset. It significantly contributes to shaping his or her experiences and responses to life's diverse challenges. This solid bond does much more than assure your child of your unwavering love. It helps foster emotional intelligence, resilience, empathy, confidence, and ultimately, a growth mindset. Understanding and effectively harnessing the emotional components of parenting can phenomenally augment a child's ability to adapt, thrive, and progress.

11.1. The Emotional Landscape of Children

Children's emotional world is a dynamic, vibrant panorama marked by rapid and pronounced changes. Understanding this landscape is crucial, for it provides a foundation upon which parents can build fruitful relationships with their kids. Children experience emotions with higher intensity than adults, primarily owing to their evolving cognitive structures and relative inexperience with emotional regulation. Hence, it is essential to validate their feelings, show empathy, and guide them toward better emotional management strategies.

Parents are often children's first interpreters of their emotional world. Labeling emotions, encouraging expression, and demonstrating healthy ways of handling emotions can help children build a robust emotional vocabulary. Explaining the nature of emotions as fluid, i.e., they come and go, can reassure children, especially when they experience negative emotions such as fear, sadness, or anger.

11.2. Building Emotional Intelligence

Emotional intelligence forms the basis of cultivating a responsive and open parent-child relationship, which in turn, reinforces a growth mindset. Parents can take active measures to facilitate emotional intelligence in their children. Here are a few ways to execute it.

1. Encourage Emotional Awareness: Carve out time for conversations centered on emotions. Intuitively inquire about their feelings and help them articulate those.
2. Promote Empathy: Demonstrate empathy and encourage your children to be empathetic towards others. Share examples and discuss empathy in daily life.
3. Teach Emotional Regulation: Teach them emotion-management strategies. Patience, deep breathing, or channeling their emotions through creative pursuits are few methods.
4. Model Emotionally Intelligent Behavior: Children observe and absorb behaviors they see around them. Exhibit emotionally intelligent behavior in your actions and reactions.

11.3. Empathy: A Powerful Tool

Empathy is incredibly influential in fostering a strong parent-child bond. It communicates to the child, 'you are not alone,' and 'I understand your feelings.' It helps nurture a secure attachment, leading to a positive self-concept and enhanced resilience- pillars of a growth mindset.

Empathy requires active listening, understanding, and responding to children's emotions, and providing comfort or guidance, as necessary. Avoid being dismissive or critical about their feelings. View conflict situations as opportunities to communicate empathy and resolve misunderstandings.

11.4. Facilitating Healthy Emotional Expression

Another cornerstone of fostering a growth mindset is facilitating healthy emotional expression. Children who learn to express their emotions authentically are better positioned to handle challenges and are more likely to grow through their experiences.

Parents can help children express emotions by incorporating simple strategies in their daily interactions.

1. Create a Safe Space: Allow children to express themselves freely without fear of judgment or punishment.
2. Model Emotional Expression: Show that it's perfectly normal and human to express varied emotions and normalize these in your household.
3. Don't Suppress Emotions: Teach children that all emotions are valid and normal. Let them know that it's okay not to feel okay sometimes.
4. Use Creative Outlets: Drawing, journaling, dancing, or even talking can be potent tools for children to communicate their feelings.

11.5. Reflection and Emotional Growth

One of the most potent tools in nurturing emotional growth is reflection. Encouraging your child to reflect upon their emotions and responses can significantly improve their emotional intelligence and resilience.

Reflective practices help children consider their emotions, understand the triggers, and strategize better responses. Reflection also promotes problem-solving skills, empathy, and emotional self-regulation. Involve your child in dialogues about their day, challenges faced, best moments, and learnings they derived from them, thereby promoting a reflective yet constructive mindset.

Cultivating a growth mindset is an on-going journey. By incorporating strategies focusing on enhancing emotional intelligence in children, parents can foster stronger parent-child relationships. The deeper your understanding of the emotional aspects of growth mindset, the more effectively can you rear a resilient, empathetic, and adaptive child ready to take on a world of endless possibilities. Remember, a child cared for genuinely and guided patiently lights up the world brighter.

Printed in Great Britain
by Amazon